SOCKS FOR THE HOMELESS

A COMMUNITY
SERVICE PROJECT

SHAY SPIVEY, BSW, MSW

Layout: Shay Mays
Cover Design: McLabz
Printed in the United States of America

Socks for the Homeless
A Community Service Project

By
Shay Spivey, BSW, MSW

See a need
Fill a need

Table of Contents

Socks for the Homeless
A Community Service Project
Indianapolis, Indiana

Website:
Socksforthehomeless.blogspot.com

Brief Summary

Who is Socks for the Homeless?
Socks for the Homeless is a community service project serving the homeless in Indianapolis, Indiana.

What
Our mission is simply to collect and distribute socks to homeless service organizations and individuals.

How
Through COLLABORATION we collect and distribute socks to homeless service organizations. Socks for the Homeless coordinates, collaborates, and partners with multiple organizations to create community service projects that collect socks for the homeless.

When
All year, every year. Community service projects like ours can be done at any time.

Where
We donate to many homeless service organizations in the Indianapolis area, but we are looking to expand to providing services to the entire state of Indiana in the near future.

Why

There are over 100 homeless service organizations in the city of Indianapolis, Indiana. Indianapolis homeless service organizations need sock donations regularly. Socks are one of the last donations that people think to give, and the organizations run out frequently. There is a constant, daily, regular need for clean dry SOCKS by the homeless community.

Also, we are the only socks for the homeless organization in Indianapolis, Indiana.

Our Values

Collaboration
Socks for the Homeless believes in developing effective partnerships with the community, businesses, organizations, and clients through professional communication, respect, service.

Customer Service
Socks for the Homeless believes in providing excellent customer service that is positive, efficient, responsive, welcoming, and friendly.

Continuous Improvement
Socks for the Homeless believes in ongoing innovation, evaluation, and growth while continuously having the courage to ask ourselves, "What can we do better?"

Socks for the Homeless

"Each morning we put on a clean pair of socks with hardly a thought. But for our community's homeless, a fresh pair of socks is often a luxury."

Friends of Boston's Homeless
www.fobh.org

About the Author

I have been collecting socks for the homeless since 2009...

I was a social work student looking for a way to personally give back to my community. I had the opportunity to interact with a lot of homeless shelters and ask about their accomplishments and challenges. When asked what they needed most, every shelter had the same response: **socks**. The homeless always needed socks, but the shelters rarely received sock donations. I decided to fill that need.

I started by contacting all my family and friends and asking for packages of socks. For Christmas I asked for sock donation in place of gifts. In addition, my daughter's school joined in the service project. Together we coordinated several school sock drives which helped to involve the students, staff, and families in a worthy cause.

Eventually, we expanded to coordinating multiple sock collection projects every year with schools, organizations, and businesses.

Give Socks
Help those in need.

Why We Collect Socks for the Homeless

Our goal is to help the homeless by providing socks through direct donations and homeless service organizations. We hope to raise awareness about the need for socks in the homeless community. We also hope to encourage more people to create, coordinate, and maintain a service projects that collect and distribute socks to the homeless in their communities.

#1

Homelessness

Homelessness is a serious problem - everywhere! Individuals and families experience homelessness for a variety of reasons and circumstances such as poverty, job loss, domestic violence, incarceration, health issues, mental health challenges, substance abuse, loss of housing, etc.

#2

Needs

Socks are just one of many needs and challenges Those experiencing homelessness have many needs, including but limited to:

Housing
Employment
Food
Healthcare
Legal
Mental Health
Substance Abuse
Education

According to The National Alliance to End Homelessness *The State of Homelessness in America 2016*, on a single night in January 2015, 564,708 people were experiencing homelessness - meaning they were sleeping outside or in an emergency shelter or transitional housing program.

To learn more check out the report at:

www.endhomelessness.org/page/-
/files/2016%20State%20Of%20Homelessness.p
df

#3

Homeless service organizations need sock donations!

There are over 100 homeless service organizations in the city of Indianapolis, Indiana. Indianapolis homeless service organizations need sock donations regularly. Socks are one of the last donations that people think to give, and the organizations run out frequently. There is a constant, daily, regular need for clean dry SOCKS by the homeless community.

Also, we are the only socks for the homeless organization in Indianapolis, Indiana.

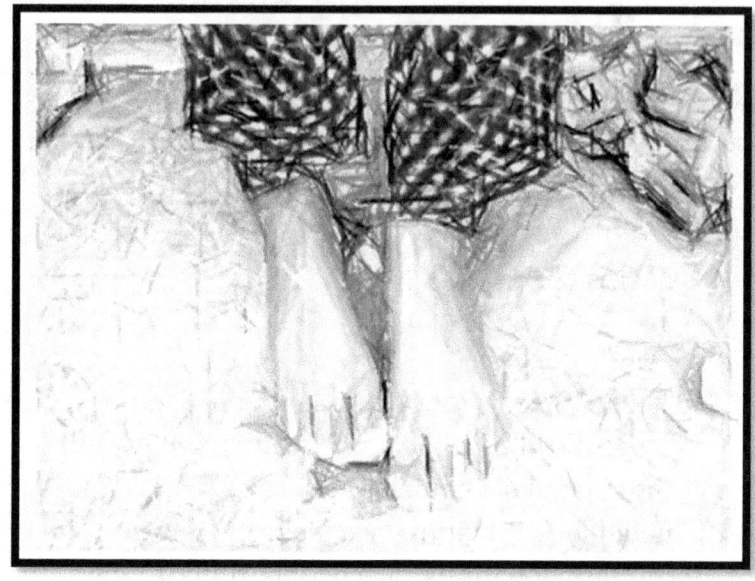

Socks for the Homeless

#4

Clean, dry socks are important

Clean dry socks offer important protection for everyone's feet - especially in extreme weather. Socks protect your feet from frostbite and provide needed warmth in cold weather. They provide padding, decrease friction and absorb bacteria causing moisture in warmer weather. Because the homeless are so mobile, their feet are put through a significant amount of stress throughout the day. A clean dry pair of the sock would help prevent a variety of problems.

Poor hygiene – limited access to showers and other washing facilities - can lead to infections and poor health. Wearing the right socks can go a long way towards good foot health.

We Can Help!

Socks offer padding, the decline in friction and moisture absorption. During the cold season, it is essential to wear socks to protect your foot from the cold, provide essential warmth, and offer anti-microbial protection. Some socks are designed with resistance qualities for bacteria.

Lack of sock protection can increase many problems, such as bacterial and fungal infections, frostbite, blisters and problems in cold weather. You can simply avoid lots of problems with the help of inexpensive socks.

Socks for the Homeless: A Community Service Project

Loading the sock boxes or delivery

#5

Mobile Population

The homeless spend most of their time walking from place to place. This constant mobility causes constant wear and tear on their feet, socks, and shoes. When your feet undergo significant stress throughout the day a good pair of the socks will make a difference to prevent foot injuries and infections.

These new socks are going to a men's shelter

#6

Continuous Need

Socks are a continuous need - people need clean socks regularly. With limited access to washing facilities the homeless wear sock for long periods of time or not at all. After long periods of use socks become thin, frayed, tattered, and a health hazard.

"The homeless put their socks through more wear and tear in a week than most socks see in a year."

Comfort Socks, 2016
www.comfortsocks.org

#7

No. 1 Needed Item

Socks are a regularly needed clothing item at homeless service organizations. Damaged socks are hard to replace because the homeless are unable to buy a new pair. Also, clothing donations to most homeless service organizations rarely include socks.

Unfortunately, socks are often an overlooked need. But that is where you come in!

When I asked what homeless service organizations needed most they all agreed - socks!

Socks for the Homeless: A Community Service Project

#8

Foot Health

Good foot care is critical.

Extreme weather can be harsh on the feet of homeless individuals, and in some cases deadly. Also, foot injuries and infections are common in the homeless community.

Health conditions like diabetes, prevalent in the homeless population, can further complicate the danger of poor foot care to include skin ulcers, infections and even tissue death. Clean socks can be just as important as medication for diabetics.

Lack of sock protection can increase many problems, such as bacterial and fungal infections, frostbite, blisters and problems in cold weather. You can simply avoid lots of problems with the help of inexpensive socks.

"See a need...Fill a need"
is the motto that keeps me
motivated to keep collecting socks
for the homeless year after year...

Socks for the Homeless
Socksforthehomeless.blogspot.com

Socks for the Homeless Organizations

In cold conditions, frostbite may happen in 30 minutes or less. Well-fitting and warm socks can help the homeless avoid any potential problem with their feet.

Homeless people may not be able to buy a new pair of socks; therefore, there are some organizations who offer new sox to needy and homeless people without any money. They conduct sox drives in schools, church groups, service clubs, colleges and anywhere else to collect new socks or funds for socks. After a drive, the new sox are collected and packed for the distribution. Socks are distributed to volunteers, homeless shelters, clinics and cafeterias for homeless people.

Following is a list of organizations that collect socks for the homeless.

Socks for the Homeless: A Community Service Project

Socks for the Homeless, Inc.

Socks for the Homeless, Inc. is a community service project the collects socks and donates to homeless service organizations in the Indianapolis area. They partner with organizations, businesses, and schools to coordinate sock drives.

Contact Information:
Indianapolis, Indiana
Contact: shayspivey@yahoo.com

Learn more at:
socksforthehomeless.blogspot.com

The Joy of Sox

The mission of The Joy of Sox is simply to provide joy to the homeless with new socks. They provide new socks for the homeless all across the United States.

Contact Information:
580 Lindsey Dr., Suite 150
Radnor, PA 19087-2339 USA
Office Phone: 610-688-3318
Fax: 610-788-2133

Learn more at:
www.thejoyofsox.org

Comfort Socks for the Homeless

Comfort Socks is a public charity that gives new socks to homeless shelters and non-profits who primarily serve the homeless population all across the United States.

Contact Information:
Comfort Socks for the Homeless
PO Box 477
Supply, NC 28462
Phone: 910-269-8577

Sock donations can be sent to:
Comfort Socks
c/o Omni Storage
4747 Old Shallotte Rd NW
Shallotte, NC 28470

Learn more at:
www.comfortsocks.org

Socks and Chocs

Socks and Chocs delivers socks, chocolates, and other needed items to homeless shelters in the British cities of Coventry, Birmingham, Wolverhampton and Worcester (England).

Learn more at:
socksandchocs.co.uk

Just Socks Foundation, Inc.

Just Socks provides new socks to the homeless of Canada. They raise funds for new sock donations to give to registered Canadian charities serving the homeless and less fortunate in Canada.

Contact Information:
388 Bloor Street East, Suite 1203
Toronto ON, M4W 3W9
Phone: 416-993-1718
Email: info@justsocks.ca

Learn more at:
www.justsocks.ca

Hope Mission's Summer Sock Drive

The Hope Mission's mission is to donate thousands of clothing items, including socks to the homeless men and women in Edmonton. You can bring socks to Hope Mission Center for your contribution.

Learn more at: hopemission.com/general-news/hope-missions-summer-sock-drive/

Socktober

They are working to provide socks to homeless and needy people all over America. They provide socks to homeless shelters and organizations.

Learn more at:
soulpancake.com/socktober

Your City Sports

They sell high-quality athletic socks and donate a new pair for homeless charity for each sold pair. They are donating socks to charities in Canada and the USA.

Learn more at:
yourcitysports.com

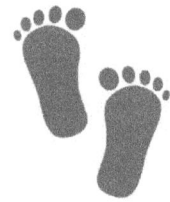

Knock, Knock Give a Sock

They provide socks for homeless people and they denote socks in Binghamton, New York City, Philadelphia, PA and New Jersey, Los Angeles and Philadelphia, PA.

Learn more at:
www.knockknockgiveasock.org/where-we-donate.html

Bombas

Bombas is an athletic-leisure sock company that partners with organizations to distribute socks to those in need. They donate all over the United States to charity organizations.

Learn more at:
www.bombas.com/giving-back

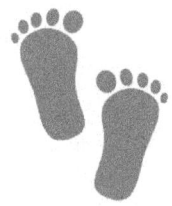

Ruby A. Neeson Diabetes Awareness Foundation, Inc.

Ruby A. Neeson diabetes foundation is a community and they collect new socks to distribute in the metropolitan Atlanta. Foot care is essential for diabetics and homeless people face difficulties in the treatment of lots of health problems.

Learn more at:
www.fightdiabetesnow.org/Sock-Drive.html

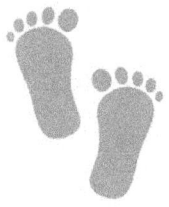

Teen Feed

The teen feed works to provide basic items and daily essentials to needy people. You can help them by providing socks and other essential items. They drop their donations on Tuesdays and Thursdays at University Congregation Church.

Learn more at:
www.teenfeed.org/blog/donate/winter-sock-basic-needs-drives-for-youth/

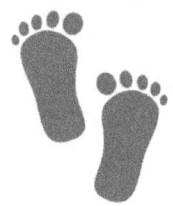

Socks in the City

They offer free socks to homeless in Australia and they are operated from 8 Cambridge Street, West Leederville,Western Australia, 6007

Learn more at:
www.socksinthecity.com.au

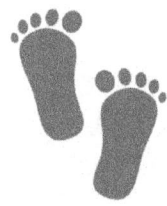

Hanes

They donate almost 200,000 pairs of socks to homeless people across the United States. You can send your donations to them for needy people.

Learn more at:
http://www.hanes.com/hanesforgood

Night Watch

They are working on a drive "Sock it to Homelessness" and you can send your new and old pair of socks to them at 21181, Seattle, WA 98111.

Phone: 206-323-4359

Learn more at:
www.seattlenightwatch.org/sockit.htm

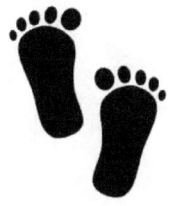

Hannah's Socks

They provide socks for homeless people to keep their feet warm and avoid health problems. It is a non-profit organization and working in Perrysburg, OH 43551.

Learn more at:
www.hannahssocks.org

Sock It to Em

They provide socks to homeless in December and you can drop socks at Susan Elizabeth Lee Ridge Plaza Dr. Castle Rock CO 80108.

Learn more at:
http://sockittoemsockcampaign.org/

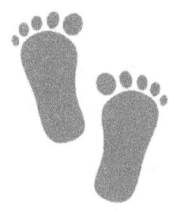

Original Jollie Goods

To keep the feet of homeless, poor and needy people, they offer socks to many homeless charities and their clients. They are registered in England to offer socks to homeless people.

Learn more at:
www.jolliegoods.com/giving

Get Involved

WE CAN NOT DO THIS WITHOUT YOU!

We hope to encourage more people to create, coordinate, and maintain a service projects that collect and distribute socks to the homeless in their communities.

We need partners like you in the community to help collect socks for the homeless. By ourselves we can have a small impact, but together in collaboration with organizations like yours we can impact thousands of lives over and over again.

The need for socks is a "recurrent need". This means that the need is constant.

Let's work together to provide this small, often forgotten, clothing article to help provide warmth and comfort to our most vulnerable neighbors!

"By organizing a sock drive at your office, school, place of worship, or even with friends and family, you not only help keep our community's homeless healthy and safe, but you also help people maintain their dignity and comfort during a difficult time in their lives."

Friends of Boston's Homeless
www.fobh.org

Project Ideas

Companies/Businesses

- Employee Sock Drive
- Community Sock Drive
- Community sock drop location

Great for team building and company community service projects.

Organizations
(Sororities, fraternities, community, etc...)

- Members and friends sock drive
- Sock drive at an event or community location

Great for community service project and volunteer hours.

Schools

- School sock drive event
- Classroom competition
- Community Sock drop location

Can include students, staff, parents, parish, and/or community

Great for community service project/volunteer hours

Churches

- Member/visitor sock drive event
- Get creative and make it an event
- Community socks drive
- Community sock drop location

Great for community service project/volunteer hours.

Individuals

- Create a sock drive at work, with family, in neighborhood, at church, etc...

Great for community service project and volunteer hours.

Checklists

Sample INDIVIDAL Project Checklist:

INDIVIDUAL

Market your socks drive - Publicize your sock drive through flyers, emails, newsletters, announcements, Facebook, or twitter.
(Hint: Be sure to include the who, what, when, where, how and why).

Collection Box – Create a large collection box. Simply print a poster and create your own collection box - Be creative.

Create a collection station - Place sock collection box in a convenient location at your home, business or organization.

Deliver – At the end of your sock collection event deliver the socks to a local homeless service organization in your area. You can find one easily on the internet.

Sample COMMUNITY Project Checklist:

COMMUNITY SERVICE

Market your socks drive - Publicize your sock drive through flyers, emails, newsletters, announcements, Facebook, or twitter.
(Hint: Be sure to include the who, what, when, where, how and why)

Collection Box – Create a large collection box. Simply print a poster and create your own collection box - Be creative.

Create a collection station - Place sock collection boxes in a convenient location at your business or organization.

Deliver – At the end of your sock collection event deliver the socks to a local homeless service organization in your area. You can find one easily on the internet.

Sample NEIGHBORHOOD Drive Checklist:

Market your socks drive - Publicize your sock drive through flyers, emails, newsletters, announcements, Facebook, or twitter.
(Hint: Be sure to include the who, what, when, where, how and why).

Collection Box – Create a large collection box. Simply print a poster and create your own collection box - Be creative.

Create a collection station - Place sock collection boxes in a convenient location or let your neighbors know that you are conducting a sock drive and will be around to collect socks for the homeless on a certain date.

Creative Suggestions - Let your neighbors know that you will set out a table/box on a certain date to collect socks for the homeless. Set up a tent, play some music, etc.

Deliver – At the end of your sock collection event deliver the socks to a local homeless service organization in your area. You can find one easily on the internet.

Sample SCHOOL Sock Drive Checklist:

Market your socks drive - Publicize your sock drive through flyers, emails, newsletters, announcements, Facebook, or twitter.
(Hint: Be sure to include the who, what, when, where, how and why).

Collection Box – Create a large collection box. Simply print a poster and create your own collection box - Be creative.

Create a collection station - Place sock collection boxes in a convenient location at your school.

Creative suggestion - Motivate students by coordinating a classroom competition and offering a prize and party for the winning class. (For example, an ice cream party, and movie party, free time, etc.)

Deliver – At the end of your sock collection event deliver the socks to a local homeless service organization in your area. You can find one easily on the internet.

Contact Shay Spivey

Thank you for reading! I would love to receive your feedback after you finish reading. Please share your thoughts about this book by leaving a review wherever you made your purchase.

Email:
shayspivey@yahoo.com

Scholarship Blog:
www.scholarshipadvisor.blogspot.com

Author Blog:
www.shayspivey.blogspot.com

Facebook:
www.facebook.com/authorshayspivey

Twitter:
@ShayMSpivey

Other Books by Shay Spivey

FREE Money for Education Series:
How to Submit a Winning Scholarship
Application: Secret Techniques I Used to Win
$100,000 in College Scholarships
How to Find Scholarships and Free Financial Aid
for Private High Schools
FREE Tuition Colleges 2016
Find FREE Money for Graduate School
FREE Tuition Colleges for Adults 50+
Understanding Scholarships and Financial Aid

Prepare for College Series:
Prepare for College: Freshman Year Checklist
Prepare for College: Sophomore Year Checklist
Prepare for College: Junior Year Checklist
Prepare for College: Senior Year Checklist

Quick Reference Series:
FREE Online College Courses for Everyone
FREE Online Art Courses
FREE Online Biology Courses
FREE Online Business Courses
FREE Online Computer Courses
FREE Online Economics Courses
FREE Online Engineering Courses
FREE Online History Courses
FREE Online Law Courses
FREE Online Math Courses
FREE Online Philosophy Courses

<u>FREE Online Psychology Courses</u>
<u>FREE Online State Programs</u>

Thank you for reading!

Other References

National Alliance to End Homelessness, (2016). www.endhomelessness.org

Friends of Boston's Homeless (2016). Retrieved from www.fobh.org

Hubred-Golden, J., (2015). Farmington Hills Bank Hosts 'Sock It to Me' Drive for NSO. Retrieved from http://www.farmingtonvoice.com/hills-bank-hosts-sock-it-to-me-drive-121900

Rivers K. (2010). Nursing students' project gather sock for homeless. Retrieve from http://www.mc.vanderbilt.edu:8080/reporter/index.html?ID=8552

When Socks Are "More Important Than Food', 2016). Retrieved from http://www.pointsoflight.org/blog/2014/06/04/when-socks-are-more-important-food%E2%80%99

www.ingramcontent.com/pod-product-compliance
Lightning Source LLC
Chambersburg PA
CBHW060411190526

45169CB00002B/855